First Edition

Paper ISBN: 978-1-938093-70-8
ePub ISBN: 978-1-938093-71-5
Kindle ISBN: 978-1-938093-72-2

Printed in China
1 2 3 4 5 6 7 8 9 10
punchline

www.punchlineideas.com

Library of Congress Cataloging-in-Publication Data

Names: Lemay, Violet.
Title: NY DOGS / by Violet Lemay.
Description: First edition. | New York : duopress, 2017.
Identifiers: LCCN 2016003793 | ISBN 9781938093708 (hardcover: alk.
paper) | ISBN 9781938093722 (mobi)
Subjects: LCSH: Dogs—New York (State)—New York—
Miscellanea. | Dogs—New York (State)—New York—Humor
Classification: LCC SF422.6.U6 L46 2016 |
DDC 636.7009747/1—dc23
LC record available at https://lccn.loc.gov/2016003793

For the Gilmores

Contents

Introduction by Jorge Bendersky   6

Prologue by Violet Lemay   9

CITY LIFE: THE BASICS   13
  1 Apartment Dwelling   14
  2 Professional Experience   20
  3 Coping Mechanisms   22

THE WALK   29
  4 Familiar Routes   30
  5 Accoutrements   32
  6 Sidewalk Perils   34
  7 In the Hood   36
  8 Fun on the Street   38
  9 Fun at the Park   40
 10 Stranger Danger   43
 11 Other Modes of Transport   44

BUSINESS TIME   47
 12 Bucket List for the Discerning Dog:
      Public Art on Which to Wee   48
 13 Poo (Number Two)   52
 14 Post-Poo Habits   53
 15 Paper or Plastic?   54
 16 The Schmear   55
 17 The Lap of Luxury   56
 18 The Big Reveal   57

BROOKLYN BISCUITS   58
(a recipe for dog treats, by Priscilla Feral)

GOURMAND   59
19   Street Meats and Other Forbidden
     Delicacies   60
20   Daily Fare   63
21   Special Treats   64

CELEBRITY   67
22   Sightings   68
23   Typecasting   69
24   Internet Sensation   70
25   The Great White Way   71
26   The Big Event Buzz   72

FASHION FORWARD   75
27   City Style   76
28   Accessories: Big Apple Chic   78

MATTERS OF THE HEART   81
29   Romantic Encounters   82
30   Secret Admirer   84
31   Soul Mate   85

PROS & CONS   89
32   The Downside   90
33   The Upside   92

ACKNOWLEDGMENTS   94

ART CITATIONS   96

Introduction
by Jorge Bendersky
Author of *DIY Dog Grooming, From Puppy Cuts to Best in Show*

New York is the result of more than 300 years of mixed races and cultures. People from all over the world and their pets settled in the area, including the three lucky dogs who survived the sinking of the *Titanic*: a Pekingese (named Sun Yat-Sen) and two Pomeranians (one named Lady and another whose name has been lost to history).

Now with more than 600,000 canine residents, New York City offers a never-ending list of pure breeds and mutts of every possible combination. Not all NYC dogs live in the fast lane,

parading around town dressed in extravagant outfits and fake eyelashes, but every single one will greet friends with a butt wiggle and a wagging tail. Dogs will make an **A-list** celebrity feel normal and a regular Joe feel like a superstar.

Every part of **NYC** has a personality that is reflected by its resident dogs and their owners. Some new developments even set aside precious space specifically for dogs to run and socialize. Despite New York's abundant array of dog runs and dog-friendly parks, plenty of pups prefer to stay home and keep a vigilant eye on their neighborhood through their apartment windows—and that's fine, too! **NYC** welcomes and accommodates every lifestyle.

NY DOGS is a love letter to not only **NYC**'s dogs and their best friends—the New Yorkers who own them—but also to the city itself. Thank you, **NYC**, for your support of the canine community!

Through the pages of *NY DOGS* and behind the artwork you will find that dogs are not only our best friends, they are New York's royal residents. **NYC** is a city that breathes dogs, admiring and protecting them with a passion and eccentricity that can't be found anyplace else.

"Outside of a dog, a book is man's best friend.

Inside of a dog it's too dark to read."

~ Groucho Marx

The Dog Who Stole My Heart: Confessions of a Former Cat Person

When I lived in **NYC** working on scenery and costumes for shows, hopping from one Manhattan sublet to another, I was a cat person.

In the beautiful, crowded chaos of New York, cats are the pet lover's obvious choice: they don't bother the neighbors, they use indoor facilities, and with the help of a timed feeding device they can even take care of themselves for a day or two. Cats easily fit into my life, and into every tiny apartment in which I lived. Mine were named Rockwell (for the illustrator) and Chelsea (for my first NYC neighborhood).

A chunk of my heart stayed behind when a career change moved me and my cats to a different city. Eventually, marriage and motherhood relocated our growing family to the suburbs. That's right: suburbia, the land of happy dogs! But in my black T-shirt, coffee cup perpetually in hand, I was still in a New York frame of mind. So what if we had a huge fenced yard? I was a cat person, through and through.

Until my son was five or six, and he and my husband began plotting.

Until they started hanging out at the local shelter and coaxing me to join them.

Until we finally found a dog who looked as if he'd never grow too big to fit through the cat door.

I distinctly remember grumbling, while signing the adoption papers, "I don't *want* a dog. Dogs always become the mom's responsibility, and I'm Mom. I already have too much to do." And just like that, I entered a clichéd relationship with a terrier-esque mutt named Chip: *The Dog and the Curmudgeon*.

We brought him home, all paws and wagging tail. As predicted, he became my responsibility. Also as predicted, I was often crabby about it. But when I wasn't cursing under my breath in annoyance, I was laughing at him, and—of course—loving him. Chip became my studio mate, my walking partner, my confidante, my in-bed foot warmer, my therapist, my constant companion, the subject of my art, the object of my codependence, my very good friend.

When business trips brought me back to my beloved NYC, I missed him. There were reminders: New Yorkers walking their dogs on each and every sidewalk, fascinating and beautiful. I sketched both dogs and walkers on napkins and bagel bags, and I called home to check on Chip at least twice a day. "Does he miss me?"

I still love cats. Apparently now I love dogs, too.

New Yorkers do life with amazing style, and their dogs have no less panache.
While Big Apple mutts come in all shapes and sizes, with personalities as
vibrant and diverse as their silhouettes, they share the uncommon
experience of living in NYC. *NY DOGS* enumerates the facts of the city dog's
life and is my tribute to the many and varied dogs of NYC—and to
the scrappy New Yorkers who, with pockets full of wadded plastic bags,
are walking at the other end of a leash.

Violet Lemay

"*Once you have had a wonderful dog, a life without one, is a life diminished.*"

~ Dean Koontz

CITY LIFE: THE BASICS

Apartment Dwelling

Unlike their suburban brethren, city dogs are apartment dwellers, which gives them a unique worldview.

Incidentally, they also happen to be spectacular window dressing.

The Brownstone

The Urban Chic

The Bohemian

While some dogs prefer to live alone (aside from their human companions, of course), taking a roommate has its advantages.

Some New York dogs even keep pets. It helps them pass the time.

After all, since living spaces are small,
visual surveillance is a breeze.

What the typical **NYC** apartment lacks in square footage, it makes up for in noise.

"Hey, I'm walkin' here!"

"TAXI!"

SCREEEEECH!!

KNOCK KNOCK

"DELIVERY!"

"外卖!"

"TAKE YOUR PHOTO?"

WOO-WOO-WOO-WO

TWEET!!

"YO!

"Shadd'up!"

HONK!

BUZZ!

The city dog's ears are always "ON."

Volunteer Dog Neighborhood Watch groups are active all over NYC. They are extremely well organized.

Professional Experience

Employment opportunities in the private sector abound for **NYC**'s talented canine work force.

The Personal Trainer

The Head of Security

The Nanny

The Cop

The Firefighter

The Guide

Some are considered among the city's upper echelon of public servants!

The Bedbug Patrol

3 Coping Mechanisms

While living in one of the world's most vibrant urban centers is glamorous and exciting, a fair amount of stress is also inevitable. Dogs in the city employ a variety of techniques to maintain their calm.

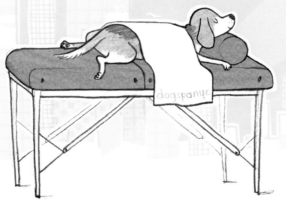

The Day Spa

Chew therapy can be very relaxing...

The Squeaky Manhole Cover and Taxi Cab

The Canvas-Stuffed NYC Icons

The Classic Rope Pretzel

The Essential Sport-Themed Tug Toys

The Posh Plush Black and White Cookie

...especially when accompanied by a chemical aid.

Watching the game helps some city dogs unwind.

Others blow off steam by pranking their owners.

The Secret Stash of Single Socks

Rooftop stargazing is a must for a city dog who is on a serious quest for inner peace.

Tranquility can also be found when the day is new and the sidewalks are quiet. Early-morning sidewalk sniffing is essential to the city dog's emotional well-being.

(Sadly, the magic of these moments is generally lost on their owners.)

"*Some of our greatest historical and artistic treasures we place in with curators in museums; others we take for walks.*"

~ Roger A. Caras

THE Walk

All dogs love walks, but for city dogs—
for whom fenced yards are far-fetched
fiction—walks are not only fun, they are
also an essential part of everyday life.

Although there are countless ways to get
from one's apartment to any point in NYC,
most city dogs and their owners establish
personal, time-tested routes that vary in
length according to purpose.

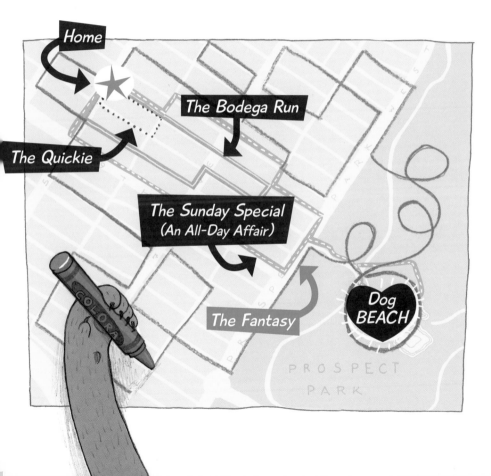

5 Accoutrements

It can take a while to get out of the apartment.
There are many accessories to gather.

The Flea Collar

(Cut to size!)

The Collar

The Flea-Repelling Collar Charm

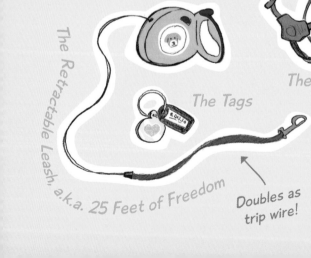

The Harness

The Tags

The Retractable Leash, a.k.a. 25 Feet of Freedom

Doubles as trip wire!

The Collection Device

The Water

The Collapsible
Water Dish

The Muzzle
(for the Especially
Friendly Dog)

The Poo Receptacle

The Ball

The Ball-Throwing
Device

Inclement weather presents special challenges...

Nope.

The Shockingly Expensive
Disappearing Boots

The Denial

...as do the sidewalks themselves!

6 Sidewalk Perils

Delicious Choking Hazard

The Chicken Bones

The Grate

The Shards of Broken Glass

The Construction Debris

The Traffic

The Spiky Heel

The Messenger

The Ferocious Lion

In the Hood

Besides providing relief for Mother Nature's perpetual call (see the next chapter!), walks broaden the city dog's social circle and generally keep life interesting.

crush

The Dog Next Door

nemesis

The Stray Cat

The Other Doorman

BFF

The Doorman

BORIS

The Homeless Gentleman

mortal enemy

unclear about this dude

The Guy with the Snake

The Nice Lady with the Pushcart

frenemy

The Mounted Policeman

not in the mood

The Delivery Person

Napoleon complex

Crazy Benny fom Down the Block

8 Fun on the Street

You never know what can happen when you're walking in NYC!

The Superhero Flyby

The Impromptu
Street Jam

The Holiday Love

The Accidental
Artistic
Collaboration

9 Fun at the Park

Dogs in the city spend lots of time in parks—some designed especially for them! Parks give the city dog a place to exercise, to relax...

The Bird Watching

The Dispensary

The Sailing

The Yoga Practice

The Sports

The Hunting

The Sprinkler Splash

41

...and to catch up with friends.

The Sisterhood

Look who's glowing!

Two more weeks, Eve.

OMG, the hair, the body... I hate her!

That's just the pregnancy talking. No wait... I hate her, too.

The Brotherhood

Jax! Where've you been, dawg?

Chasin' tail.

Yo' mama's tail!

It's inevitable that passersby would be attracted to the city dog's cuteness; however, inequity in the dog community re: social skills is not uncommon.

The Love Muffin

The Ongoing Gentrification Project
a.k.a. the "Sociopath"

Other Modes of Transport

While walking is a transportational mainstay for every city dog, other options are available.

The Airport Shuttle

The Cab

The Mass Transit System

The Tram

The Limo

The Sherpa

The "Toto"

"*Dogs are the leaders of the planet. If you see two life forms, one of them's making a poop, the other one's carrying it for him, who would YOU assume is in charge?*"

~ Jerry Seinfeld

BUSINESS TIME

Bucket List for the Discerning Dog:
Public Art on Which to Wee*

Amazing public art abounds in **NYC**.
Who could blame a dog for wanting
to mark such precious territory?

The Wonderland Wee

The Haring Challenge:
A Triple Dog Dare

The Picasso of Pee

13 Poo (Number Two)

Unlike their country cousins whose backyard "packages" are collected rarely, if at all, every product of the New York dog is collected, wrapped, and processed as soon as it arrives.

The Traditional "Soft Serve"

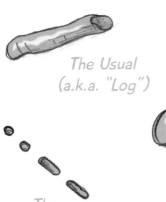

The Usual (a.k.a. "Log")

The "Kibbles-n-Bits"

The Personal Masterpiece

The Morse Code

The Horrible Mush
a.k.a. The Free Pass— because who could pick it up?

Post-Poo Habits

City dog physiology can, at times, include some rather strange behavior.

The Sudden Bolt

The Scoot

The Kicky Dance
Learned it from the cat

15 Paper or Plastic?

Dog owners in the city never leave home without one of these handy collection devices.

The Classic

The Boutique Assortment

The Serious Collector

The Improv

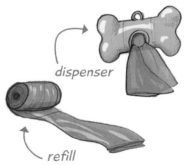

dispenser

refill

54

The Lap of Luxury

Some lucky New York dogs don't have to bother with any of this nonsense, especially when the weather is unpleasant.

LAWN LOO

The Big Reveal

18

In the spring, melting snow reveals a winter's worth of preserved poo, providing a host of compelling sniffing opportunities.

The excitement is contagious...and a little exhausting.

BROOKLYN BISCUITS

Recipe courtesy of Priscilla Feral, from the book **For the Love of Dog Biscuits***

2-1/2 cups whole wheat flour

2 Tbsp. golden flaxseed meal

1/2 cup canned pumpkin

9 Tbsp. water

2 Tbsp. all-natural peanut butter

1 tsp. ground cinnamon

Preheat oven to 350°. Mix all ingredients in a bowl. Knead the dough until workable (should be somewhat dry and stiff), and roll to a 1/4" thickness. Use cookie cutters to cut shapes and lay them 1" apart on a cookie sheet lined with parchment paper or on a silicone baking mat.

Bake for about 25 minutes, until light golden brown. Cool the cookies on a rack before serving. Store in airtight container in the refrigerator or freezer.

*DOG KARMA: All proceeds from *For the Love of Dog Biscuits* (available at fortheloveofdogbiscuits.com) go toward Friends of Animals spay/neuter campaign.

GOURMAND

Street Meats and Other Forbidden Delicacies

With enticing aromas wafting from every corner, New York, New York is a gastronomist's dream! This presents a certain amount of frustration for the average city dog.

Being surrounded by out-of-reach temptations
might sour the disposition of a lesser beast,
but NYC dogs are tougher than most.

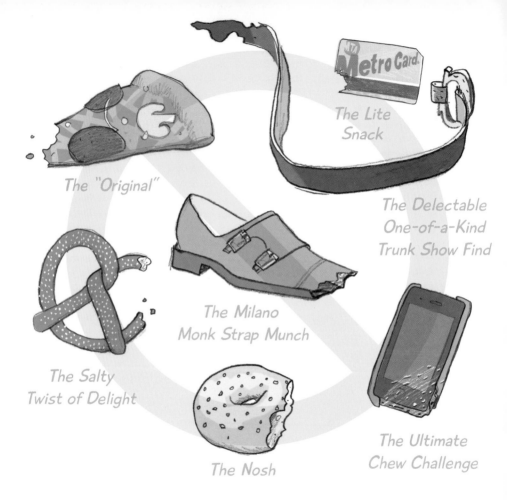

The "Original"

The Lite Snack

The Delectable One-of-a-Kind Trunk Show Find

The Milano Monk Strap Munch

The Salty Twist of Delight

The Nosh

The Ultimate Chew Challenge

Safety requires some dietary restrictions, but it's all good.

The Alfresco Brunch

The Local Watering Hole

The Takeout

City living includes a variety of lovely dining options.

The aforementioned "toughness" of NYC dogs doesn't preclude their ability to enjoy the finer things that their city has to offer.

Never fear! No matter how fancy
the treats in which they occasionally
indulge (organic, gluten-free, artisanal,
made-from-scratch), dogs in the city
never adopt a bourgeois attitude.

"Every dog must have his day."

~ *Jonathan Swift*

CELEBRITY

Sightings

As a cultural hub, NYC is crawling with canine stars of print, stage, and screen.

Isn't she the model from those ads?

The Cover Girl

The Big Top Bow-WOW

Even the most diverse, bicoastal, agent-represented, method-trained pooch can't avoid being pigeonholed.

Don't look so smug, Lassie—you haven't got a chance.

If they make me wear a sombrero, I will go full Cujo on their asses.

CASTING
SPOKESDOG
FOR
Tia's Tacos

Chihuahua, please.

I played Lear in the Park (behind the trash cans) for #$%&'s sake! LEAR!

24 Internet Sensation

Dogs in the city make regular appearances across all social media outlets, but they don't let it go to their fuzzy little heads.

So, this is for *The Dog Blog?* Cool!

Her name is Foxy. She's a rescue.

Instapix

dashjack   24 days

foxyfox129 #doxierocks

#DOXIEROCKS

Not even the glitter of Broadway can affect a city dog's disposition! NYC's pooch A-listers are a very well-grounded group.

NYC dogs know how to put on a show!
In February, tails wag as purebreds of the highest
pedigree compete for Best in Show.

In June, ears twitch and hearts leap as NYC dogs bark it up in Shubert Alley for the Best of All Causes: pet adoption!

"Dogs are the fashion because we can fashion them to our will."

~ Quentin Bell

FASHION
FORWARD

27 City Style

Whether dressed for a special event or a bodega run, dogs in the city always look fabulous...

Le Film Noir

The Boho Chic

The Masquerade
Perfect for the NYC Halloween parade, Greenwich Village, or Tompkins Square!

The Black Tie

Mermaid Parade
Coney Island

The Seaside Fantasy

...and no dogs represent like New York City dogs!

Looking good 24/7 is hard work.

Beauty rest is essential.

Trend Alert:

COLLARS & TAGS

The Bad Girl
All sugar, no spice?
Go hard-core with this
spikes-n-skull combo.
Finally: respect!

The Princess
Nothing's too good for
our sweet baby.

The Sleek Sport
With no tell-tale tag jingle, this bespoke nylon
number makes pigeon hunting a breeze.

Bandana Basics
Do-Rags for City Dog Swag!

The Urban Cowgirl
City chic meets country classic.
"'Merica, y'all!"

The "Too Much Pink..."

...said nobody, ever! Go feminine and get your tail chased. (Note from the Editor: You're welcome!)

The Big Apple Betty
Tie-dye brings the breeze of Saturday's surf into your Monday Gotham romp. Mahalo, mutt!

"The only creatures that are evolved enough to convey pure love are dogs and infants."

~ Johnny Depp

Romantic Encounters

Big Apple dogs are lovers, for sure! With beautiful breeds on display in every dog run and park and on every sidewalk, there's no shortage of arrows in Cupid's quiver.

Sometimes, it doesn't work out.

Love can be confusing...

...and some things just weren't meant to be.

Behind New York City's millions of windows, there are bound to be a few lovelorn peeping toms...

...and yes, even the occasional voyeur.

Soul Mate

Whether or not city dogs find love within their own species, they never suffer for lack of affection.

NYC dogs and their owners share a special bond.

I get the shoe fetish, but WHY DID YOU EAT MY SCREENPLAY?

[kiss kiss kiss]

You're right, Cupcake, it was dreck. Forgive me?

The Puppy Love

A kiss at the Lipstick Building

The Unconditional Love

The Love That Makes Life Worth Living

Sure, sometimes it can get a little weird...
but hey, this is New York!

The Transference*

...and I had that dream again.
You're the only one who
really gets me, Magda.
God, I really love you!

The "Baby"

Good listener

* Patients often fall for
their therapists!

The Twins

a.k.a. "The Narcissism"

"Owning a dog is slightly less expensive than being addicted to crack."

~ Jen Lancaster

PROS & CONS

Of course, life in the city presents challenges for dogs...and for their owners.

Besides the energy one must expend
to maintain status as a good neighbor
while simultaneously owning a dog,
there is—alas—the ledger
to consider.

The Culprit

The Existential Crisis

a.k.a. "Cone of Shame"

The Finder's Fee

The Emergency

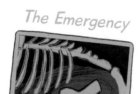

sock ↗

The Big List

Gonzo: Expenditures

Adoption Donation
Immunizations
Neuter surgery
Extra Pet Security Deposit
Giant Bag-o-Puppy Chow
Bowls & food
Bed for front room
Bed for back room
Collar & Tags
Vet & de-worm meds
Urine-b-gone
Anti-pee spray
Noleen flea
new toys
Couch re-stain
Couch re-upholster
OBEDIENCE
Dog-training
Dog Walker
New Cap
Anti-
Couch

The Perpetual War "Man vs. Flea"

Still, though. Just look at that face!

"Such short little lives our pets have to spend with us, and they spend most of it waiting for us to come home each day. It is amazing how much love and laughter they bring into our lives and even how much closer we become with each other because of them."

~ John Grogan

Acknowledgments

No book by Violet Lemay would be complete without a drawing or two contributed by her son, **Graham Fruisen**, who drew the map of Park Slope and Prospect Park on page 31. Thank you, Graham!

Violet's husband, **Fred Fruisen**, not only designed *NY DOGS*, he also proved his self-appointed "Funny Guy" nickname by tweaking his wife's words to make them "funnier," "better," and "less boring." Violet says, "Thank you, Baby. Now please, stop."

Violet would also like to thank her friend and indefatigable profanity coach **Doreen Chila-Jones** for her many and varied contributions to this project. Doreen's comedy stylings, quick wit, and general smart-assedness shaped words as well as many of the concepts behind the art in *NY DOGS*. Dor even snapped the photo that inspired the "Mass Transit" illustration. She's basically a godsend and possibly also a genius, although we're keeping that quiet so as not to wreck her sweet and humble demeanor.

Thanks also to **Jane Seymour** and **Friends of Animals** for allowing us not only to reprint **Priscilla Feral**'s recipe on page 58, but also to rename it! In the book *For the Love of Dog Biscuits*, "Brooklyn Biscuits" are titled "Pumpkin-Flaxseed Biscuits." To order, go to fortheloveofdogbiscuits.com. DOG KARMA: All proceeds benefit the Friends of Animals spay/neuter campaign. Woof!

We are grateful to our social media followers who contributed photos of their dogs to inspire Violet, who placed them here and there throughout *NY DOGS*—among a flurry of fictional pups and a few actual NYC A-listers.

The Cast of *NY DOGS*, in order of appearance:

★ Finlay McBoo ★ Chip ★ Rocky* ★ Chelsea* ★ Bose ★ Oliver ★ Ralph ★ Boom Boom ★ Coco ★ Ollie ★ Tank ★ Lucy 1 ★ Apricot* ★ Layla ★ Dalton ★ Jack ★ Chloe Belle ★ Baggins ★ Grover ★ Lúlú Dior ★ Cody ★ Peaches ★ Tapa† ★ Leo* ★ Gio ★ Rocky ★ Button ★ Bear ★ Dolly ★ Jester ★ Chelsea ★ Chowser ★ Missy ★ Wilson ★ King Creole ★ Baer ★ Trix ★ Mr. Jones ★ Miss Foxy Brown ★ Morty ★ Nora ★ Tommy ★ Dexter ★ Riley ★ Ranger ★ Oreo ★ Scout‡ ★ Sonova Winter Born Lady ★ Petunia ★ Bogart ★ Buckeye ★ Prada ★ Lucy 2‡ ★ Katie ★ Iryss ★ Bentley ★ Brody ★ Dakota ★ Gonzo† ★ Angus ★ Bullet ★ Lady† ★ Yofi† ★ Rosie ★

* A cat!

† Tapa is featured five times in *NY DOGS*, usually from behind. It's all about that fluffy tail!

‡ These are all litter mates whose owners still meet for playdates. So nice!

A special thank you to our favorite city for its constant support of all things eclectic, cultural, and artistic; in particular, thank you **NYC** for letting us poke a little fun at the following glorious works of public art:

p. 48 *Alice in Wonderland*, a bronze sculpture in Central Park, by José de Creeft, 1847

p. 49 *Concrete Jungle*, a temporary mural on the Bowery Graffiti Wall at the intersection of Houston Street and the Bowery, by Futura, 2015

p. 50 *Crack Is Whack*, a mural on a handball court at 128th Street and Harlem River Drive, by Keith Haring, 1986; *Self Portrait*, a sculpture at 51 Astor Place, and *Two Dancing Figures*, a sculpture at 17 State Street, both by Keith Haring, 1989

p. 51 *Bust of Sylvette*, a concrete enlargement of a sculpture by Pablo Picasso in Greenwich Village by Carl Nesjär, 1967

p. 82 *Balto*, a bronze scuplture in Central Park, by Frederick G. R. Roth, 1925